How To Deal With
Difficult
People

Revised Edition

How To Deal With
Difficult People

by Paul Friedman

SkillPath Publications, Inc.
Mission, Kansas

Editor: Kelly Scanlon

Cover and Book Design: Rod Hankins

Cartoons: Charlie Podrebarac

ISBN 1-878542-77-X

Contents

Introduction 1

1 What Makes People Difficult? 3
Exercise 1: Identifying Your People Network 4
Exercise 2: Identifying Difficult Behavior and Setting Goals 6

2 Changing Difficult Behavior 11
Exercise 3: Blaming Patterns 14
Exercise 4: Analyzing the Problem 16
Exercise 5: Implementing Your Own Plan 22

3 Preventing Difficulties 23
Exercise 6: Strategies for Preventing Difficulties 40

4 Being the Solution, Not the Problem 41
Exercise 7: Identifying Your SAGs 51
Exercise 8: Overcoming SAGs 54

5 Difficult Modes of Talk 55
Exercise 9: Communication Modes 59

6 Encouraging Desirable Behavior 65
Exercise 10: Tracking Positives 68
Exercise 11: Messages of Praise 72
Exercise 12: Conditional Appreciation Messages 75

7 Summing It Up 77

Bibliography 79

Introduction

Management expert Peter Drucker once wryly remarked, "Working with people is difficult, but not impossible." That's also a basic thesis of this book. It's certainly obvious that many people are *difficult* to deal with, but after reading this book, you won't find them *impossible.* You'll be empowered to understand behavior patterns better and establish good working relationships with even the most frustrating individuals. Best of all, the information the book provides is short on theory and long on *practical* interpersonal techniques you can put to work immediately.

As new information is introduced, highlight, underline, or bracket ideas that you can use when dealing with the difficult people *you* encounter. Then apply those ideas directly and immediately to your interaction with the difficult people you deal with at work.

To help you put the ideas in this book to use, exercises are inserted periodically. These exercises allow you to clearly think out strategies for dealing with the difficult people you know and to anticipate their possible reactions—before you approach them. You may wish to copy these exercises or to write your responses on another sheet of paper so you can redo the exercises each time you are faced with a "difficult people" situation.

By applying the guidelines in this book, you should see a definite improvement in your interpersonal skills in general; in particular, you will find that you are making progress toward achieving specific goals with the difficult people in your life.

What Makes People Difficult?

IDENTIFYING DIFFICULT PEOPLE

Let's get off to a flying start with an exercise for identifying the difficult people in your life. Begin by thinking of all the people you deal with regularly in the course of a typical day. Exercise 1 consists of a chart you can use to quickly map your "people network." Think of yourself as being in the center. Each of the peripheral circles represents one of the people you interact with. Fill in their names (just their initials will do). You needn't use every circle, and you can add more circles if you wish to include more people. You also might put a *group* of people in a circle — the accounting department, impatient customers, and so on.

Exercise 1:

Identifying Your People Network

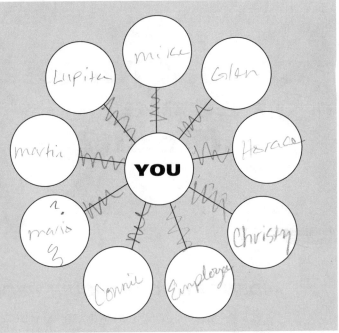

Next, assess the degree to which you have difficulty dealing with each of the people on your chart. Mentally review your recent interactions with each person. Sense within yourself the degree to which you are satisfied with that relationship. On the line that connects your circle with the other person's, indicate the degree of satisfaction or "difficulty" you experience.

- Use angular diagonals to indicate the people you experience difficulty with.

- Use smooth, curving lines to indicate the people you interact satisfactorily with.

Satisfactory Relationships = $\wedge\!\wedge\!\wedge\!\wedge\!\wedge\!\wedge$
Difficult People or Groups = $\vee\!\vee\!\vee\!\vee\!\vee\!\vee$

Your chart might look something like this:

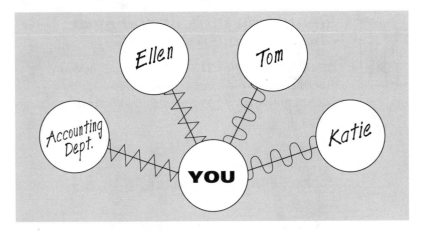

This diagram now reveals at a glance the people you have most difficulty relating to and those you communicate with best. You can learn quite a bit by analyzing both kinds of relationships.

DESCRIBING DIFFICULT PEOPLE

Describing difficult people usually is more elusive than naming them. It may not be easy for you to express in words what people do that bothers you, or what you would prefer that they do instead.

So, use Exercise 2 to specify a few of the things the most difficult people in your life do or don't do. These descriptions will provide you with a clear definition of the problem situation(s) you are facing. It is important, too, to specify exactly what you would prefer those people to do. Identifying what you want provides clear target(s) to shoot for.

Exercise 2:
Identifying Difficult Behavior and Setting Goals

For each person you have difficulty relating with, describe a behavior you find difficult to handle. Then write down what you wish that person would do instead.

1. Person _Lupita_

   A behavior I find difficult to handle is _Chaotic - Too much Changing her mind - not being consistant_

   I wish that person would _Not expect so much Stay w/ what she says_

2. Person _Mario_

   A behavior I find difficult to handle is _too laid back_

   I wish that person would _Do his work_

3. Person _Horace_

   A behavior I find difficult to handle is _too friendly - it makes me nervious - does he have alterior motives_

   I wish that person would _treat me normal so I could stop worring._

4. Person *Christy*

A behavior I find difficult to handle is *lies + acts like everyone else is doing her wrong*

I wish that person would *Own her own life.*

5. Person *Glen*

A behavior I find difficult to handle is *Selfish —*

I wish that person would _____

6. Person _____

A behavior I find difficult to handle is _____

I wish that person would _____

7. Person _____

A behavior I find difficult to handle is _____

I wish that person would _____

DIFFICULT TYPES

In his well-known book *Coping With Difficult People,*
psychologist Robert Bramson identifies several types of
difficult people. Compare his typologies to the difficult people
you deal with:

- *Hostile-aggressives* bully and overwhelm by bombarding
  others, making cutting remarks, or throwing tantrums
  when situations don't go the way they think they
  should.

- *Complainers* gripe incessantly but never do anything to
  resolve what they complain about.

- *Silent and unresponsives* respond to every question and
  every plea for help with a yes, a no, or a grunt.

- *Super-agreeables* are very reasonable, sincere, and
  supportive in the presence of others. But they don't
  produce what they say they will, or they act contrary to
  the way they've led others to expect.

- *Negativists* object "It won't work" or "It's impossible"
  when a project is proposed. All too often they deflate
  any optimism others might have.

- *Know-it-all experts* are "superior" people who believe
  and want others to recognize that they know everything
  there is to know about anything worth knowing. Such
  people are condescending, imposing (if they really do
  know what they're talking about), or pompous (if they
  don't). Often they make others feel like idiots.

- *Indecisives* stall major decisions until the decisions are
  made for them. They can't let go of anything until it's
  perfect—which means never.

Did you find any of your difficult people in Bramson's
typologies?

One shortcoming of Bramson's list is that it categorizes and labels people. Many people prefer instead to speak about what's difficult in terms of specific *behaviors* or *incidents*. Every day each of us does something that someone finds difficult. But that doesn't make us all "difficult people."

CATEGORIES OF DIFFICULT BEHAVIOR

Everyone does something that irks other people. But most people change when told that their behavior is irritating or inappropriate. Communication researchers Craig Monroe, Mark Borzoi, and Vincent DiSalvo define difficult behavior as what people do *despite corrective feedback from their employer.* They asked 381 managers, from nine widely varying organizations, to think of one male and one female employee who fit this definition and to describe a recent example of their behavior. The managers' responses were divided into these four categories of difficult behavior:

- *Apparent compliance* (mentioned by 40%). The employee appears to accept negative feedback from a superior, promises to change, and then reverts back to the typical pattern of difficult behavior.

  Example: "If I've told Mary once, I've told her a thousand times, to check the procedure manual before filling out requisitions. She always apologizes all over herself and promises to do it next time. She continues to goof up. I swear she just doesn't listen."

- *Discouraging word* (mentioned by 21%). The employee refuses to accept the superior's feedback.

  Example: "Dan has been with this agency for twenty-five years. In the seven years I've been here, he has criticized every change we've tried to make.

His standard line with me and the others is 'When you have been here as long as I have, you'll learn that this kind of thing won't work.' I respect his experience, but I'm tired of being made to feel like a snot-nosed kid."

- *Alibis* (mentioned by 20%). The employee transfers responsibility for problems elsewhere.

   Example: "My assistant manager knows he is responsible for managing inventory. It's in his job description. Whenever I mention it to him, though, he has an excuse: 'I'm tired,' or 'I'm overworked,' or 'That should be John's job.' I'm sick of it."

- *Avoidance* (mentioned by 19%). The employee absents himself or herself from the scene.

   Example: "When trouble arises, Mark can't be found. One time last year he took two weeks of sick leave right after his performance appraisal. I guess he may have been sick, but this is typical of him. I doubt that he really was sick."

Clearly, many people must deal with some basic forms of difficult behavior every day. Note that the difficult behaviors in the examples could occur in *any* organization. None were profession-specific, position-specific, or gender-specific. Human relations problems crop up wherever people must work together. As Theodore Houser once wrote, "It's not the hundred-and-one problems of production and distribution that keep executives awake at night; it's the problems of working with people, the human problems of their job." Focusing attention on difficult behaviors, specifying what they are, and identifying how they might be changed—as you have in this chapter—are key steps in handling them.

Changing Difficult Behavior

2

You can do much to influence the people around you. Before labeling someone "difficult," it's only fair to be sure you've done your best to change that person's behavior. The person could simply be oblivious to your discontent or underestimate it and assume you really don't mind. Changing someone's difficult behavior involves several factors.

YOU HAVE GOT TO BE KIDDING...

FRAMING THE PROBLEM

First, you must analyze how you are "framing" the problem—how you think about it and how you describe it. Believe it or not, the way you think about and describe a problem affects how people respond to it. The greatest danger is simply imposing your own "cause-effect" sequence on what occurs. Behavior occurs in an *ongoing stream*—"life is just one darn thing after another" as the saying goes. People tend to impose on that stream their own interpretations of what is "cause" and what is "effect," often without fully understanding what has occurred "upstream" or how their interpretation and handling of the situation will affect what happens "downstream."

Recall, for example, the worker in the first chapter who didn't fill out requisition forms correctly. Her boss is likely to assume she is responsible for her own performance (and, of course, say she is). The worker might justifiably claim, however, that the procedures manual is confusing (she has a point). The writer of the procedures manual believes that the instructions are clear but that people must be given hands-on training (oh, so that's the real cause). The training manager might say the employee was trained properly but must complete too many bureaucratic, red-tape forms and, therefore, is forced to neglect the requisitions form (aha, now we've uncovered the really real cause). The division manager might say that all the company's forms are absolutely necessary and that the problem lies with the worker's immediate boss, who is being too critical and impatient in his feedback to the worker (now we've returned to where we started). Obviously, we could go on and on, adding other possible causes and effects.

Could all of these explanations be correct? They could be.

If so, who must change to solve the problem? Any one of the parties mentioned could make a difference. Each person and procedure is an element in a *system,* and each affects the others. Change in any one element will change what's occurring in the system. If this is so, no one element is exclusively at fault; none is the cause, none is the effect. No one person should be labeled the villain, no one the victim. All can be viewed as either cause or effect; all may be deemed involved and "responsible." All are possible avenues for change.

What does this "system analysis" imply about changing difficult behavior?

First, it should guide your thinking about the purpose of a change process. It's not for blaming and labeling. However, it *is* for identifying:

- The dysfunctional system.

- The elements of the system that could be affecting the difficult behavior.

- Alternative actions that might alter the system.

- The likely consequences of each action.

- The action most likely to have the desired impact.

- How to carry out that action.

Second, a system analysis minimizes the likelihood that someone will feel hurt, angry or embarrassed when discussing the situation or that you and the difficult person will become embroiled in a debate. Bitter feelings and conflict usually arise only when dealing with a difficult person is viewed as a struggle for supremacy, for determining who will win and who will lose, for identifying who is right and who is wrong. When you eliminate accusations, you reduce the emotional upset of both parties.

Third, reframing the cause-effect model can help you involve the difficult person in handling the problem. You may view people as the "cause" of their own difficult behavior. But as you saw in the "alibi" category in Chapter 1, many people project cause outward and may even see you as the "cause" and themselves in the "effect" position. If so, they're likely to place responsibility for what they're doing and the need for change on you. If you view the problem from a cause-effect frame, you'll feel resentful and debate their claim.

Rather than dispute who is at fault, you're better off if you simply acknowledge that things aren't going as they should. Then ask:

- How *should* things be run?

- What can *each of us* do to bring that about?

People are more likely to carry out whatever plans are made if they are involved in the decision-making process.

Exercise 3:
Blaming Patterns

Consider how you are framing the behaviors you find difficult. Think of any difficult behavior you listed in Exercise 2. Then say aloud all four of the sentences below, filling in the difficult behavior where the underline occurs.

Difficult behavior _____

1. I am to blame for <u>(the difficult behavior).</u>

2. He (or she) is to blame for _____.

3. We both are to blame for _____.

4. No one is to blame for _____.

Which sentence do you believe is (a) most true, (b) most satisfying to you, and (c) most conducive to constructive dialogue about the problem?_____

Are you beginning to see how the way in which you frame a problem affects the way the other person responds? How you respond?

SITUATION—TARGET—PLAN

Once you understand how you are framing a particular problem behavior, you can set about changing the behavior. Changing someone's difficult behavior involves bridging a gap between the current *situation* and what is preferred, or the *target*. How do you bridge the gap? By devising a *plan* to facilitate the change. By completing Exercise 2, you've already taken the first step in identifying the current situation and setting a target behavior. However, as you've just learned, no situation is ever an island unto itself. All behavior is embedded in a system, or "real-world" context. To develop a realistic plan, you must not only identity the situation, you must identify, or frame it, within its larger context.

Identifying the Situation

Here are some of the factors you must consider as you try to identify any "difficult behavior" situation:

- Does the situation have a history? Have previous attempts been made to resolve the situation?

- You and the other people involved have limits on what you are willing and able to do to resolve the difficult behavior. How much time, resources, or authority do each of you have at your disposal?

- What forces keep the person in his or her current mode of behavior?

Exercise 4:
Analyzing the Problem

Think about the problem behavior you identified in Exercise 3 and check the appropriate answers in the spaces provided here. Your answers will guide you in developing an appropriate plan to handle the problem.

1. Does the difficult person have the *ability* to achieve the goal? Could that person, if his or her life depended on it, reach the target? ☐ Yes ☐ No

   The question of ability determines whether the difficult behavior is an issue of *motivation* (has the ability) or *skill* (lacks the ability).

2. If your answer to Question 1 is "yes," ask:

   (a) Is achieving the target specifically *rewarded?*
       ☐ Yes ☐ No

   If you answered "no," a plan for changing the situation is now evident—you should provide *clear* and *positive consequences* for achieving the target.

   Write them here:

   _____

   _____

   _____

   _____

   _____

   _____

   If you answered "yes," go on to item b.

(b) Does achieving the target bring *negative consequences?*
☐ Yes   ☐ No

Or is *not* achieving it rewarded?
☐ Yes   ☐ No

Sometimes people are criticized by their peers for going along with what the boss wants. Or, sometimes people fear that doing more work will cost them their job. Both of these are negative consequences for doing better work.

If your answer to either of the questions in item b is "yes," your plan should be to *improve or alter the consequences of achieving the target.* For example, you might separate the person from the people who discourage doing better work or relieve the person's concern that improvements could bring penalties.

Write some ways for improving the consequences for achieving the target:

_____

_____

_____

_____

_____

_____

_____

_____

_____

_____

3. If your answer to Question 1 was "no," ask:

  (a) Has the person ever reached the target *before*?
      ☐ Yes   ☐ No

   If the answer is "no," the person needs *training.*

   If the answer is "yes," ask these two questions:

  (b) Does the person perform the target behavior incorrectly?
      ☐ Yes   ☐ No

   If the answer is "yes," the person needs *constructive feedback.*

  (c) Has the person performed the target behavior recently?
      ☐ Yes   ☐ No

If the answer is "no," the person needs *practice.*

Now write down some ways to train, provide constructive feedback, or offer practice—whichever the person needs:

_____

_____

_____

_____

_____

_____

_____

_____

_____

_____

You can see from this exercise how important it is to understand fully the current situation before devising a plan for achieving the target.

Developing a Target

The target statement you wrote in Exercise 2 is only a start toward remedying the difficult behavior. The target must be something that *both* you and the difficult person view as desirable. If you're the only one who wants to achieve the target, you'll meet resistance all along the way. As long as a person feels frustrated, coerced, or required to "sacrifice" to accomplish the target, some resentment will linger and grow, eventually undermining the entire effort.

Hence, the target statement must include factors that allow everyone to feel satisfied or achieve a "win/win" solution. Let's go back to the difficult person (a salesman) in the first chapter who predicted that every change proposed by his younger boss would fail. The boss might set a target of getting the salesman "to agree to back up his new program ideas." That would be a "win" solution for the boss. However, the salesman, who truly feels pessimistic about his boss's changes, would regard this target as a "loss" and agree to it only under duress. How could the manager set a target that *both* would regard as a "win"?

He would try to devise a target that takes into account the salesman's concern. The salesman thinks that anything different than the status quo is doomed to failure. The target, then, would have to include that concern as a possibility rather than to rule it out. It also would have to include the manager's optimism about his program suggestions so he feels like a "winner" too. A mutually satisfactory, win/win goal might be that "both manager and salesman agree to cooperate in a trial run of the next new program idea to see whether it works." This is a target both parties might agree to without feeling a "loss."

Such a target is specific and can be measured reasonably. It would be even better to identify in concrete terms what "cooperate" means and to set a specific date for assessing achievement of the target.

Devising a Plan

The plan includes the precise steps or the path to be followed when moving from the situation to the target. Often there are many alternatives for achieving a target. Hence, it makes sense to explore several approaches and not simply to adopt the first one that comes to mind. Nor should you commit too soon to any one way of doing things. When reviewing a possible plan, ask yourself whether:

- It is likely to achieve the target.

- It is practical. Is the plan viable within the constraints of the situation?

- The people affected by the plan are willing and even excited about carrying it out.

As mentioned previously, it is helpful to involve the "difficult person" in developing the plan. Ask the person to devise the plan or to choose a plan from two or three that are acceptable to you. Involving the "difficult person" in the choice usually elicits from that person a greater commitment to carrying out the plan successfully.

Once the plan is established, each person must understand clearly what he or she has agreed to do, by *when,* and in what *form.* Checkpoints should be included along the way to ensure that the plan is being implemented as agreed. Sometimes the issue to be resolved is not *what to do* but *who is to perform* a function. If this is the case, consider a process developed by the Federal Mediation and Conciliation Service. The process, called Relationship by Objectives (RBO), is most useful when two parties disagree on who is to do what.

The first step involves having each person list (either orally or in writing) four different sets of activities:

1. I think I should...

2. You think you should...

3. I think you should...

4. You think I should...

Try to phrase your statements positively rather than negatively ("He should stop doing..." becomes "He should start doing...").

Next, working together, condense the two lists into one—the activities you both can agree on. Pick the goals you believe deserve the highest priority and decide how to achieve them. Outline, step by step, what has to be done, when each step should be accomplished, and who will be responsible for seeing it through.

To understand how this method might be applied in a specific situation, recall any instance from the past when you and someone else (a "difficult person") disagreed about the assignment of tasks—that is, when one of you felt taken advantage of, overburdened, or imposed upon.

Then carry out the RBO process yourself, filling in what you think you and the other person thought each should do at the time. Recall how you actually handled the situation. Then consider how much better your interaction would have been—how much freer of difficulties—had you used this simple process.

Following the full Situation—Target—Plan procedure ensures that you've done your part to change the "difficult person."

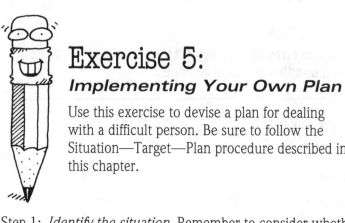

Exercise 5:
Implementing Your Own Plan

Use this exercise to devise a plan for dealing with a difficult person. Be sure to follow the Situation—Target—Plan procedure described in this chapter.

Step 1: *Identify the situation.* Remember to consider whether the situation has a history as well as what your limitations and the difficult person's limitations are. _____

_____

_____

_____

_____

Step 2: *Set a target.* Remember to make it a "win/win" situation for both you and the difficult person. _____

_____

_____

_____

_____

_____

Step 3: *Devise a plan.* Include precise steps for reaching the target.

_____

_____

_____

_____

_____

Preventing Difficulties

DIFFERENCES VS. DIFFICULTIES

If everyone thought and acted alike, there would never be any difficulties between people. We'd operate in perfect harmony. Difficulties arise only among people who see the world and tackle problems *differently*. Many people, therefore, try to surround themselves with similar, like-minded, agreeable people. Avoid differences and you avoid difficulties. Right?

Perhaps. But when you shun differences, you also lose a lot. Differences add spice to life. Different perspectives bring fresh ideas, creativity, and innovation. Without differences, an organization is composed of mere "yes-men." An organization without differences is like a superhighway crossing a flat plain: smooth and boring. An organization that welcomes differences is like a road that twists through a mountain range: difficult to traverse, but exhilarating and varied.

MAINTAINING GOOD WORKING RELATIONSHIPS

Yes, differences are valuable and appealing, but they are accompanied by difficulties. From this perspective, difficult people are more challenging than people who are like you, but that challenge is worth tackling. One of the keys to dealing with difficult people, therefore, lies in developing good working relationships with people who are different from you.

How do you develop these good working relationships? Harvard professors Roger Fisher and Scott Brown provide several suggestions in their book *Getting Together: Building a Relationship That Gets to Yes.* Here are some of the major points they make:

- Separate relationship issues from substantive issues.
- Be unconditionally constructive.
- Beware of partisan perceptions.
- Balance reason with emotion.
- Inquire, listen, and understand.
- Consult before deciding.
- Be trustworthy.
- Use persuasion, not coercion.
- Accept and deal seriously with people.

Separate Relationship Issues From Substantive Issues

When people at work disagree, two outcomes are in doubt:

1. What decision will be reached

2. How the individuals will feel about working together in the future

The first question involves the *substantive* issue, how the *content* of the dispute will be resolved. The second involves the *relationship* issue, how the *individuals will deal with each other* as people.

You can win at one level and lose at the other—get what you want substantively, yet make an enemy. Or vice-versa—you may not obtain what you want substantively, yet strengthen a working relationship.

To disentangle the two issues, explicitly separate your working relationship with the other person from whether you agree with or approve of that person's viewpoint. That means thinking, "I will treat this person well whether or not I like what that person thinks or does."

The United States maintains embassies and communicates regularly with officials in many nations—despite disapproving of various policies some of these nations have. So, if someone at work seems difficult, you might say to yourself:

> *I can and will maintain a decent working relationship with that person, although I don't like what that person does. Our relationship doesn't imply that I agree or approve of that person's behavior. Like governments all over the world, I can keep open lines of communication with people I regard as difficult or even as enemies. That's the only way improvement can ever occur. It's possible and sensible to disentangle substantive and relationship issues.*

Be Unconditionally Constructive

Many people deal with difficult people in the same way those people treat them: by reciprocating what they receive. This may be called an "eye-for-an-eye" policy. If the other person yells at them, they yell back. If the other person snubs them, they ignore the other person. If the other person insults them, they insult that person right back. If the other person cheats them, they cheat the other person.

The eye-for-an-eye policy is based on a traditional approach to justice. Unfortunately, in a modern organization, it is largely ineffectual, even dangerous. Why? The "victim" often is damaged as much as the perpetrator. Reciprocation sets off a negative spiral.

If A lies to B, and B deceives A, what is A likely to do next? Tell the truth? Unlikely. More than likely, A will lie again—but more cleverly this time.

If A threatens B and B counterthreatens, what is A likely to do? Capitulate? Hardly. Instead, A will probably present a more severe threat or carry out the original threat.

Reciprocation doesn't resolve anything. It doesn't cure A of being difficult. It just elicits *more* of the same difficult behavior, and it converts B to A's style of relating. A negative, escalating, mutually destructive cycle of difficult behavior is generated.

What's the alternative? Being *unconditionally constructive*. That is, being committed to forging a good working relationship whether or not the other person reciprocates.

You might think that this is a ridiculous solution. Why should you be considerate and constructive when someone else is simply being difficult? There are several reasons. The most important is that it pays off for *you*. Consider your alternatives:

How to Deal With Difficult People

- If the difficult person is being irrationally angry, are you better off responding angrily or responding reasonably? (If you respond angrily, all you produce is a heated battle. If you respond reasonably, you're less likely to do something rash or foolish.)

- If the difficult person won't listen to you, are you better off ignoring that person or trying to understand him or her? (The more you listen to and know about that person, the less you "shoot in the dark" for a solution and the more effectively you deal with the person.)

- If the difficult person breaks a promise to you, are you better off breaking your own promises or keeping your word? (If you keep your word, you remain trustworthy and your words will have more impact.)

A good friend of the black educator Booker T. Washington tells of a time when he and Dr. Washington were walking down a city street together. A passerby recognized Dr. Washington. The man's face turned mean, and he deliberately bumped into Washington, uttering a racial slur as he did.

The friend was livid. He asked Dr. Washington: "Aren't you going to retaliate? Give him a tongue lashing!"

Washington smiled patiently and replied: "No. I refuse to let any man cause me to hate."

Washington was determined not to let someone else's behavior, especially a bigot's, determine his own. He insisted on remaining in charge of his own thoughts and behavior, on not following the eye-for-an-eye policy. He chose to be unconditionally constructive.

Beware of Partisan Perceptions

Each of us sees the events of our lives and other peoples' behavior from our own vantage points. Thus, we see only "part" of the whole. (Recall the systems analysis approach in the section on "framing" behavior in Chapter 2.) We tend to think, nevertheless, that our perspective is accurate and representative of what's occurring.

Unfortunately, there are at least two sides to every story and many ways to view every incident. At the end of a hard week, for example, a boss and an employee reflect on life in their organization. Each sees things a little differently.

The employee laments, "There's too much paperwork in this organization." The boss complains, "People are always late with their monthly reports."

The employee thinks, "If I were boss, I'd have some control over my life." The boss thinks, "My employees have no idea how much pressure I'm under."

The employee believes, "My boss doesn't trust me—he's always looking over my shoulder." The boss believes, "I'm breaking my back to spend time with my people and train them."

The employee thinks, "My boss doesn't appreciate what I do." The boss thinks, "My employees don't appreciate what I do."

Where you stand on an issue depends, therefore, on where you sit. In other words, how you think about people depends on your position. When we judge difficult people, we often forget that our perceptions of them are only partial. Yet we defend, or become "partisans," of our perceptions.

There's much that people do that we don't see. There are interpretations of our own behavior that we don't consider. A company president once took a visitor on a tour of corporate headquarters. On the grounds was a fish pond. The president said he used it to screen job candidates.

The visitor asked, "How?"

"I ask them to look in the fish pond and tell me what they see," the president replied. "If they see fish, I hire them. If they see only their own reflection, I don't."

The company president knows that people who are entranced with themselves and their partisan perceptions become poor managers. Those who see other people and understand their viewpoints are more effective.

Balance Reason With Emotion

We all know that in some instances too much emotion can diminish performance. The person who is very agitated when taking a test or giving a speech performs poorly. A person who becomes furious at a child who commits a minor transgression hurts rather than helps the child. A person who fears going to the dentist feels the pain from a toothache escalate.

On the other hand, an organization with little or no emotion is dull and lifeless. Some experts say that the most effective leaders are extremely emotional—and even act as cheerleaders—about the goals they're trying to achieve. For example, an appropriate amount of emotion helps energize a speaker.

But responding impulsively and emotionally to a difficult person usually only worsens the relationship, especially if the person is making you angry. A good working relationship with a difficult person requires a reasonable approach. What can you do to balance emotional and rational reactions to behavior that upsets you? Fisher and Brown have several suggestions:

- *Take a break.* Ask for a short recess. Go for a walk, get a drink, or otherwise interrupt your buildup of emotion. You might even ask to adjourn your meeting and arrange to reconvene on another day.

- *Count to 10 if an official break isn't possible.* That disrupts your upward emotional spiral and gives you a chance to rethink the situation.

- *Consult a third party.* If you feel heated about your relationship with someone, ask for a reaction from a neutral party.

  Consider the following anecdote. A client once told his lawyer about some litigation he was considering. He asked the lawyer, "How would that case stand up in court?" The lawyer smiled and responded: "No problem. You're sure to win." The client thanked him and started to leave. The lawyer said, "Wait, don't you want me to pursue the case for you?" The client replied: "Nope. What I just told you was the other guy's side of the story."

- *Acknowledge and talk about your emotions.* Say, "Excuse me, but this is beginning to make me angry." Or explain precisely what is upsetting you:

  "This is frustrating me. When I tried to explain my plan for this account, I was interrupted in midsentence.

When I tried to be constructive and suggest that we bring in a consultant, your response—if I recall correctly—was 'Can't you handle this yourself?' What's going on?"

- *Accept responsibility and apologize if an argument erupts.* Say: "I regret that we're having this misunderstanding, and I'm sorry for my part in it. If I have misinterpreted what you were saying or done anything to upset you, I apologize." Such a statement makes it easy for the other person also to accept a portion of the responsibility and to agree to move on to a more reasonable approach. It is mature and constructive, not weak or passive, to accept responsibility for an argument you're involved in rather than to resort to blaming.

- *Prepare yourself when you know an emotional situation is likely.* When a lawyer knows a client will be cross-examined about a stressful event, the lawyer alerts the client beforehand so that the client is braced and ready, rather than surprised and upset, on the witness stand. Likewise, you might think about how you want to act in an upcoming encounter with a difficult person and actively elicit the appropriate emotions within yourself.

Say you're worried that you might feel critical and angry with a difficult person. You'd prefer to be open-minded and optimistic. You can "recruit" the latter feelings by picturing in your mind how you'd like to act—that is, by mentally rehearsing the attitude you want to have. You also can dress, stand, and practice statements that are consistent with your preferred attitudes. With those rehearsed thoughts fresh in your mind, you're more likely to feel and come across as cool, calm, and reasonable in the stressful situation.

Inquire, Listen, and Understand

Every year in this country, thousands of companies merge with or are acquired by other companies. A shockingly high percentage of these mergers fall far short of their financial goals. The predominant reason is that people in the acquiring company don't really understand the people, the processes, or the culture of its new partner. The lesson? We can't deal effectively with difficult people unless we understand them. Unfortunately, however, people usually overestimate their understanding of others.

When you feel that someone is being difficult, it's always best to assume there's a good reason for the behavior—a reason that you don't yet understand. In an interview with *Psychology Today,* psychologist George Miller said, "In order to understand what another person is saying, you must assume that it is true, and try to imagine what it's true of." Unfortunately, most people assume that what other people say is absurd or untrue and try to imagine what could be wrong with them to make them say anything so ridiculous.

The Japanese have an apt story that illustrates how important it is to be open to inquiry, to listening, and to trying to understand. An American tourist visited a Zen monastery and asked the abbot to explain Zen philosophy to him. The abbot could tell from the American's manner that he already thought Zen to be merely a quaint, archaic, bizarre way of life, so he asked the visitor to join him for a cup of tea. The American was annoyed at this delay, but agreed nonetheless. The abbot set out two cups. He poured tea into the American's cup until it was full, and then continued pouring. The American shouted, "Stop, you can't fit any more tea in there—it's just spilling over the side!" The abbot smiled and replied: "Ah, and that's what would happen if I tried to explain Zen to you. Your mind is already full of preconceptions. You have no space to receive what I would say. My words would simply pour over the sides. Empty your mind. Become open to learning, and then we can speak meaningfully."

In the same way, we must first empty our minds of preconceptions about difficult people. We must not assume we understand them. We must ask ourselves, "What do they care about?" Studies by Harvard psychologist David McClelland, for example, indicate that people are primarily motivated by one of three things:

1. *Achievement*—the desire to do interesting work and do it well

2. *Affiliation*—the desire to form good relationships with people

3. *Power*—the desire to achieve status and influence

Many people who are motivated by achievement think that affiliation-oriented people are lazy socialites and that power-oriented people are do-nothing bureaucrats. People motivated by affiliation might think that achievement-oriented people are workaholics and that power-oriented people are heartless. People who want power may view the other two types of people as spinning their wheels and getting nowhere. People who jump to these types of conclusions forget that other people may have different interests and desires—"march to a different drummer," so to speak—than they do.

A student once asked a professor to teach him the secret to the art of conversation. The professor said she'd be glad to. The student waited. The professor remained silent. The student finally blurted out, "I'm listening." The professor replied, "Aha, now you know!"

Consult Before Deciding

When people work closely together, what one person does usually affects the others. (This interdependence certainly applies to members of a family as well.) Yet we often make decisions or take actions without consulting or even notifying the people who will be affected by these actions and decisions. Unfortunately, this usually upsets the people who are kept in the dark and destroys good working relationships.

Why do we sometimes neglect to consult those affected by our actions? Usually, it simply doesn't occur to us, or we assume there's no need for it. Perhaps we think we already know what the other person will say. Or we're sure we've made the right decision and feel we have the authority to make it. So we just "tell" the other person what we've done and expect that person to accept it.

But people don't like being controlled by others, even if what's decided is in their own best interests. People like to participate in decision-making, even if they would have made the same decision anyway. So it's best always to consult anyone who will be affected by any of your decisions.

This doesn't mean giving up your right to decide, however. Consulting merely involves letting someone know that you are considering and soliciting input about a particular matter and that you are taking that input seriously. When you consult others before making a decision, they feel as if you see them as important, as meaningful players in the decision-making process. When people don't feel coerced into accepting a decision, they are more understanding and accepting of the decision. Consulting others before deciding leads to being appreciated rather than to being viewed as a difficult person.

Be Trustworthy

Working relationships are better among trustworthy people. People who can be counted on to keep their word are trustworthy. Trustworthiness is not an objective measure of honesty and reliability. It is a qualitative measure. If I *believe* you will do what you say, then I perceive you as trustworthy. If I suspect you won't, your credibility with me is low.

Faith in people is fragile. Once broken, it's hard to restore. You may think: "I have good intentions. I usually come through with most things I promise. I'm not trying to hurt anyone. I should be trusted." But being trustworthy in three out of five instances doesn't earn trust. Every single breach of trust diminishes people's confidence in you. Even if you keep your word nine out of ten times, others will remember the one time you didn't and wonder when you will disappoint them next. (Many people's trust is as disproportional as the man who told the dictionary author, "You're disgusting. I've read your book and there are at least ten instances of profanity in it!")

Sometimes we make promises carelessly—when we say, for example, "I'll be home by 6:00" without checking our afternoon calendars. Or we treat promises lightly, saying "Don't worry, I'll take care of that" to reassure someone and then neglect to follow up in the press of other events. Sometimes we tell little white lies, such as "I never got the message" or "I tried to reach you" to someone we should have called back. These apparently insignificant breaches of trust gradually erode our credibility and encourage others to indulge in their "difficult" behavior.

Most people believe themselves to be more trustworthy than others think they are. We forgive ourselves more readily for minor transgressions that linger in other peoples' minds. *We* know why we neglected to do something. *We* know we had a good reason and intended no harm. But others can't read our minds or know what our lives are like. All they know is they've been let down. And to them we're "difficult" people.

We can improve our trustworthiness by taking our promises seriously and making an effort to fulfill them—by being on time for appointments, for example. Also, when we know ahead of time, we can warn people about obstacles that are likely to interfere with our ability to keep commitments. We also can honestly admit, explain, apologize, and offer to do whatever it takes to compensate for our broken commitments when they do occur.

We can help other people be more trustworthy as well. We shouldn't tempt people too much by "overloading" them with trust. If someone leaves money lying around and people take it, who is at fault? Not just the thief. The person negligent with the funds is guilty of "trust overloading." Most firms hire auditors to go over their books, not because the firms suspect their employees of stealing, but because that precaution keeps opportunities for violating trust to a minimum.

Society abounds with examples of "trust control." Banks seek collateral on loans, landlords collect security deposits when renting apartments, and customs inspectors examine the luggage of overseas travelers. All do so to keep trust within manageable bounds. Likewise, you can help unreliable employees be more trustworthy by incorporating more "auditing procedures" into their work—by more frequently checking their progress and performance.

Be wary, too, of "underloading" people with trust. Peering over peoples' shoulders in perpetual distrust damages their trustworthiness. Backseat drivers don't help youngsters develop their own driving judgment. If you frequently suspect someone of unreliable behavior, you eventually create a self-fulfilling prophecy—that person begins to think dishonesty is normal and expected. To avoid trust underloading, many businesses have employees perform their own quality inspections rather than use quality inspectors. Separating production from quality control had created, in many cases, a division between the two functions. Producers thought "What can I get away with?" and inspectors thought "What can I catch?" If you assume people don't care about their work, soon they won't.

When untrustworthy behavior occurs, we must control our anger. Perhaps we're overreacting based on our own perceptions and biases. What you may view as intentional betrayal may be mere forgetfulness or a misinterpretation of expectations. Or you may be giving your own needs higher priority than the other person does. (A mother once was asked how her children's marriages were going. She replied: "My daughter married a wonderful man. He buys her expensive gifts, takes her on lavish vacations, and brings her breakfast in bed. My son married a terribly selfish woman. She expects expensive gifts, lavish vacations, and breakfast in bed!")

Treat disappointing or difficult behavior as a *joint problem*, not as a crime. When someone doesn't do what you expect, don't simply accuse or blame. Ask "What can *we* do to be sure this doesn't occur again?"

Use Persuasion, Not Coercion

When people are being difficult and you have more authority than they do, it's tempting to *force* or *coerce* them to do as you wish. But compliance through coercion—such as threatening harm—provides only short-term gains and long-term losses. People resent being coerced and eventually express that resentment in angry outbursts or acts of revenge. Coercion creates competition to see who will "win," and methods to create win/win solutions are overlooked. Rather than resolve difficulties, coercion usually just perpetuates or escalates them.

A difficulty should be seen as a problem that both parties wish to solve through cooperation. Both should be on the "same side of the line," attacking the *problem,* not *each other.* Managing difficult behavior is not a contest; it's a challenge to invent a solution both people support and feel committed to implementing.

To do this, neither party can afford to adhere to only one way of handling the problem. An either/or, "take it or leave it" approach usually creates a standoff or results in one party coercing the other or giving up in despair. Remember the story of the two frogs thrown into the center of a huge vat of milk. One looked around, couldn't see the rim, gave up on survival, sank to the bottom, and drowned. The other, thinking there had to be a way out of the predicament, kept swimming. By morning he was standing safely atop the pile of butter his churning had created.

If people continue thinking, talking, and attempting to persuade each other of what's best, the law of requisite variety will begin to apply. That law, paraphrased from the world of cybernetics, states that the person who has one more alternative than the number of obstacles he or she faces eventually will triumph. In other words, "where there's a will (and available alternatives), there'll be a way."

Accept and Deal Seriously With Difficult People

It's tempting to scorn and reject people who don't fulfill our expectations. When disappointed, we become critical and disdainful. We slam the door on communication and give up on problem solving.

But we have to remember that the action that upsets us is only a small part of the difficult person's constellation of behavior. Consider, for example, the advertising executive who mishandled an account and had to report it to his board of directors. He started his talk by posting in front of the room a large sheet of white paper with a small black dot on it. He asked the board members to tell him what they saw. They said, naturally, "A small black dot."

The executive said: "Yes, and there's also a large white sheet of paper. Notice that when something is blemished, we attend to that small blemish and overlook the broad background on which it is placed. I hope you'll keep that background in mind when I make my report this morning."

The difficult behavior of many people is simply a small dot on a large background. Be sure to keep that background in mind. Let the offending person know you are aware of his or her positive qualities. Even if the person is a support worker, he or she is equally a human being and worthy of basic respect. Treating people with acceptance and respect, even if their behavior is difficult at times, provides the groundwork for improvements.

Exercise 6:
Strategies for Preventing Difficulties

Review the prevention strategies discussed in this chapter and complete the following sentence:

To better prevent difficulties with my co-workers and to build good working relationships with them, I will:

_____

_____

_____

_____

_____

_____

_____

_____

_____

_____

_____

_____

_____

_____

_____

_____

Being the Solution, Not the Problem

When two people don't get along, each usually blames the other for the problem:

- "He started it!"

- "I'm doing the best I can."

  - "What else can I do when she acts that way?"

Do you ever think similar thoughts? Most people do. When self-justifying thoughts are running through your mind, what do you suppose other people are thinking?

The same thing, of course!

They assume *you're* the cause. You assume *they're* the cause. And the war goes on.

You each believe things would be better if only *the other person* would change. You certainly can *try* to change difficult people. But think about your own past experience: Have you ever found it easy to change someone? Probably not. People resist being changed.

THE IMPORTANCE OF CHANGING YOU

Unless people are willing to change, change is unlikely. You can't reach into their minds and change how they think. In truth, the person you can control most readily is *you.* You have direct access only to your *own* thoughts, body, and speech.

When you change, other people also are likely to change voluntarily. Why? Because people behave differently in different situations. So when you change your behavior, others naturally adapt themselves to your new behavior.

Don't you communicate differently with each of these people—your boss, support workers, best friend, worst enemy, small child, an elderly person, doctor, door-to-door salesperson, police officer, and so on? The common denominator in all your communication situations is you. Yet your behavior differs somewhat depending on the individual you are communicating with. What variable alters your behavior? Primarily, it's how the other person treats you!

So, if you treat difficult people differently, they will respond differently—and probably not be so difficult any more. Keep in mind that the difficult people you encounter usually think you're the one who's being difficult. When asked to explain their difficult behavior, difficult people usually say they're acting in response to you. So, if you change, other people no longer believe they have reason to be difficult.

SAGS AND SAPS

You may still be thinking that you know some truly difficult people—they're simply difficult individuals and what you do is irrelevant. Perhaps that's so. But, unfortunately, many people inadvertently "trigger" in other people the difficult behaviors that bother them most.

Here are a few examples:

Max has been reserved in the group for several meetings. When he finally speaks, he feels hurt when the others don't pay much attention to his suggestions. (Who's the "difficult" party—quiet Max or the impervious group members?)

Jackie is overburdened with work, yet she almost invariably says "yes" when her colleagues request her assistance. (Who's really difficult—agreeable Jackie or her demanding co-workers?)

Ted is authoritative and patronizing with the women who work for him. He's suddenly shocked to learn that sweet, petite Linda has been quietly manipulating him into making a fool of himself. (Who's more difficult—macho Ted or manipulative Linda?)

All three of these individuals probably feel they're dealing with difficult people. Actually, they're engaging in self-defeating behavior—they're eliciting from other people the behaviors they find difficult to handle. Donald Bowen of the University of Tulsa calls these communication patterns *Self-Annihilating Games,* or SAGs for short. And he calls SAG perpetrators SAPs, for *Self-Annihilating Person.*

A SAG is a repetitive, self-maintaining, unsatisfying pattern of communicating in which at least one party, the SAP, is both the initiator and the victim. Everyone practices a SAG or two. SAGs are frustrating, but normal—not an indicator of a character flaw or mental illness.

A SAP needs *collaborators*—and the SAP often characterizes these collaborators as "difficult" people. Sometimes these collaborators clearly behave unpleasantly—for example, they may yell, but only after the SAP has yelled first.

Sometimes the SAP only imagines the collaborator's behavior—a salesperson who *imagines* a customer will slam the door in his or her face may not make a call.

Here's the usual SAG sequence:

1. The SAP has a negative self-image or a negative image of other people and behaves in a way reflecting that image, starting the SAG.

2. The collaborator(s) perceives that behavior and reacts "logically," given the SAP's behavior.

3. The SAP perceives the collaborator's actions, labels them "difficult," strengthens his or her original negative image, and intensifies the SAG behavior.

Here's an example. In his book *Working,* Studs Terkel reports the comments of Larry Ross, a retired executive who views the business world as a jungle. Ross says: "The executive is a lonely animal in the jungle who doesn't have a friend…Deep down, they're scared stiff. The fear is there. You can smell it. You can see it in their faces. I'm not so sure you couldn't see it on my face many, many times during my climb up."

Ross starts the SAG sequence, then, with the belief that people in business are aggressive predators, and it's scary to him. Ross continues: "You're always on guard. Did you ever see a jungle animal that wasn't on guard?" And he is contemptuous of trust: "The most stupid phrase anyone can use in business is loyalty." Believing the best defense is a good offense, he manages his support workers by fear: "I always said, 'If you do a good job, I'll give you a great reward. You'll keep your job.'"

If Ross sees all his support workers as disloyal, self-seeking, untrustworthy jungle animals waiting to pounce on him if he makes the slightest slip, it's understandable that he views himself as unsafe and untrusted and reinforces this image in every interaction with his support workers.

Let's trace Ross's thinking in our three-step model:

1. He thinks: "Everyone's out to get me. I'm in constant danger." His behavior is hostile and distrusting.

2. His employees see him as hostile, dangerous, threatening, and exploitive. So they react "logically" by protecting themselves, withholding information, telling him only what he wants to hear, and undermining him when they can.

3. Ross perceives their behavior, feels confirmed in his belief that they're difficult and dangerous people, and escalates his own manipulative management style.

Ross created the difficult people who worked for him.

Do you recognize yourself or people you know in the following SAGs?

SAG #1: The Wallflower

SAP's Self-Perception: "I don't have any ideas or experiences others will find interesting."

SAP's Behavior: Is very quiet and reserved; hangs back during meetings and social occasions

Collaborator's Perception: "Wallflower doesn't have much to say."

Collaborator's Logical Reaction: Ignores Wallflower; interrupts or tunes out Wallflower

SAP's Perception of Collaborator's Difficult Behavior: "What a cold, uncaring, aloof person. Obviously someone not interested in me."

SAG #2: The Scaredy-Cat

YES. NO. MAYBE. GET BACK TO ME NEXT YEAR.

SAP's Self-Perception: "If I speak frankly and openly about myself, I might look foolish and be vulnerable."

SAP's Behavior: Makes only small talk and doesn't bring up anything personal or important

Collaborator's Perception: "Cat seems superficial, closed, distant, and uncomfortable talking about feelings."

Collaborator's Logical Reaction: When Cat's around, makes small talk; doesn't raise topics likely to make Cat uncomfortable

SAP's Perception of Collaborator's Difficult Behavior: "These people are uptight. They speak on the surface and seem unwilling to become personal friends. They're probably cold fishes, purely out for themselves."

SAG #3: The Pollyanna

SAP's Self-Perception: "If I say anything negative, peoples' feelings will be hurt, and they'll become upset."

SAP's Behavior: Shares only positive feelings; is always polite, formal, and courteous

Collaborator's Perception: "Pollyanna doesn't seem strong enough to deal with strong feelings or negative reactions."

Collaborator's Logical Reaction: Avoids confronting Pollyanna or bringing up anything unpleasant

SAP's Perception of Collaborator's Difficult Behavior: "I was right. They can't deal with reality. They never say what they really think."

SAG #4: The Macho Man

SAP's Self-Perception: "If I don't prove I'm a real man, people will think I'm a wimp."

SAP's Behavior: Acts super-tough; super-masculine

Collaborator's Perception: "M-M is one tough, mean hombre."

Collaborator's Logical Reaction: (Men): Compete with him to show I'm as much a man as he is; (Women): Flatter and manipulate M-M

SAP's Perception of Collaborator's Difficult Behavior: "You've got to be tough in a world where most people are trying to compete with you or manipulate and exploit you—and the rest are wimps."

SAG #5: The "Fluffy"

SAP's Self-Perception: "It's a man's world and a woman needs someone to take care of her."

SAP's Behavior: Is passive, self-deprecating, flattering to men, doesn't take women seriously

Collaborator's Perception: (Macho Man): "My kind of woman." (Others): "What a bubblehead."

Collaborator's Logical Reaction: Macho Man pursues her. Others distrust, discount, or take advantage of her.

SAP's Perception of Collaborator's Difficult Behavior: "I'd better stick close to Macho Man or these other people will run right over me."

SAG #6: The Underdog

SAP's Self-Perception: "I feel powerless and that frightens me."

SAP's Behavior: Does whatever people in power want (dependent) or does only what people in power don't want (counterdependent)

Collaborator's Perception: (of Dependent Underdog): "What a yes-man." (of Counterdependent Underdog): "What a nut."

Collaborator's Logical Reaction: Ignores or takes advantage of Dependent Underdog; avoids or attacks Counterdependent Underdog

SAP's Perception of Collaborator's Difficult Behavior: "It just goes to show how little power I have around here."

SAG #7: The Egotist

SAP's Self-Perception: "People are fascinated by me, and they aren't very effective if I don't help them."

SAP's Behavior: Boastful, self-centered, domineering

Collaborator's Perception: "What a fathead. I'd better just go along—Egotist never listens."

Collaborator's Logical Reaction: Listens politely; tolerates Egotist's delusions

SAP's Perception of Collaborator's Difficult Behavior: "They worship me. They wouldn't know what to do without me."

SAG #8: The Old Softy

SAP's Self-Perception: "If I'm really nice to people, they'll love and appreciate me."

SAP's Behavior: Unable to say "no"; disorganized and overworked; can't prioritize because he or she doesn't accept validity of own needs

Collaborator's Perception: "Old Softy's awfully nice, but not very effective."

Collaborator's Logical Reaction: Overloads Softy with unimportant tasks, but avoids delegating important assignments or promoting Softy to key positions

SAP's Perception of Collaborator's Difficult Behavior: "See, they do appreciate me. They keep giving me more to do."

SAG #9: Mr. Spock

SAP's Self-Perception: "If we start expressing feelings, I could lose control of myself and the situation."

SAP's Behavior: Emphasizes rationality; avoids "emotions"

Collaborator's Perception: "Spock doesn't care how I feel."

Collaborator's Logical Reaction: Deals with Spock only in rational, businesslike terms; suppresses emotions of excitement, irritation, fear, warmth, and so forth

SAP's Perception of Collaborator's Difficult Behavior: "I need to increase my control of this situation because these people don't have their hearts in it."

SAG #10: The Perfectionist

SAP's Self-Perception: "If my work isn't perfect, I'll appear mediocre or foolish."

SAP's Behavior: Compulsive perfectionism; avoids errors at any cost; overworked and overstressed

Collaborator's Perception: "I sure don't want to work for Perfectionist," or "Perfectionist gets things done right no matter what."

Collaborator's Logical Reaction: Avoids being evaluated or controlled by Perfectionist or assigns toughest jobs to Perfectionist

SAP's Perception of Collaborator's Difficult Behavior: "They give me all the tough, dirty jobs to do, but not enough help to get them done."

Exercise 7:

Identifying Your SAGs

Review the ten SAG examples in this chapter. Do you
find yourself in any?

_____

_____

_____

_____

If you do, relate that SAG to the "difficult" behavior you identified
in Exercise 3. Do you somehow generate the behavior you dislike?
If so, what change in your own behavior is likely to reduce the
difficult behavior of the other person?

_____

_____

_____

_____

_____

_____

_____

_____

_____

OVERCOMING SAGs

How can SAGs be overcome? Here are some suggestions:

- *Awareness.* Just being aware that you might play a role in someone else's difficult behavior helps you be alert for the SAG and minimize its occurrence.

- *Feedback.* SAPs who aren't aware they are triggering a SAG need to be told that they are doing so. Even after people recognize their roles in an ongoing SAG, they may not be aware of the behavior that set the SAG in motion and, therefore, continue to exhibit the behavior. Such people may need feedback—a warning or a "yellow caution light"—from another person involved or from an onlooker.

- *Support.* Because changing a customary way of dealing with people can be unsettling, the SAP may need support. But the type of support needed may vary from person to person. Some people prefer a tough-minded scolding each time they return to their old ways. Others prefer gentle reminders and encouragement. The person changing should identify which type of support he or she considers more helpful.

- *Alternative behaviors.* Sometimes a SAG continues because the SAP simply doesn't know any other way to handle the situation. Bowen gives this example, a variation on the "Old Softy" SAG. Sue, a bright and conscientious woman, was personnel manager for a chain of fast-food restaurants. Her "difficult" people were the other managers (all male) who ate lunch together. When they left for a restaurant, rather than invite Sue along, they would ask her to listen for any important phone calls they were expecting. Sue wanted to be invited to lunch, but she felt that asking would be "too pushy."

Bowen asked Sue to do a "role-reversal," to imagine she was in her male colleagues' shoes. He played her part and said, "It bothers me that you guys leave me to watch the phones while you go to lunch. The secretaries could easily handle the calls, and I'd like to participate in your discussions of how we run this place." Sue felt that approach was reasonable. She now had an alternative to her situation. She tried it, and was readily included in the lunch group. Sue managed the difficult people at her job by frankly revealing her own thoughts about the situation.

A 1985 study of executive self-development published by the Center for Creative Leadership indicates that SAGs present crucial challenges for moving ahead in organizations. Researchers interviewed twenty-two executives and found these common barriers to their career growth:

- The power of the position makes others afraid to give them feedback.

- Their orientation to action discourages introspection.

- Their need to appear competent makes it difficult for them to accept criticism.

- Their history of success makes it difficult for them to recognize the need to change when old ways are no longer appropriate.

These findings indicate that managers, especially, need to ask themselves this question: "Am I doing something to *create* the difficulty I'm facing?" Questioning your own behavior can be one of your best defenses against difficult people.

Exercise 8:
Overcoming SAGs

Which of the suggestions for overcoming SAGs applies to you? Write down how to use that suggestion for overcoming a SAG.

_____

_____

_____

_____

_____

_____

_____

_____

_____

_____

_____

_____

_____

_____

_____

Difficult Modes of Talk

It's easy to deal with someone who wants what we do and does what we want. We usually consider people "difficult" only when we disagree with them. But conflict isn't always unpleasant. You probably know several people who act and think differently than you do, but you like and respect them anyway.

Why, then, do we experience some people as difficult when we conflict with them? The explanation lies in how they *express* their different viewpoints. Certain modes of expressing an opinion are especially annoying. They evoke negative emotions in listeners, and those emotions give rise to hostile responses that exacerbate the conflict.

OUTTA MY WAY!

MODES OF COMMUNICATION

In her book *The New People Making,* psychologist Virginia Satir identifies five ways people air their opinions when disagreement exists:

- Blaming
- Placating
- Computing
- Distracting
- Leveling

The more people are under stress, the more consistently they employ their customary mode of self-expression. See if you can identify which mode is most characteristic of the difficult people you know.

Blaming

People who use the Blamer mode assume they are right and you are wrong. They are innocent and you are guilty. They are good and you are bad. They exaggerate what's going on by using words such as "every," "always," "never," "nobody," and "nothing" to make accusations or threats. They give orders. Their body language is threatening. They shake their fingers or bang the table. They frown and scowl. They speak loudly or talk through clenched teeth. They also stress key words very strongly: "You simply don't CONsider what ANYbody else in the firm might want. You ALways do things YOUR way!"

Placating

People using the Placater mode are overly eager to avoid offending anyone. They praise excessively ("How wonderful!" or "That's really great!"). They plead and cajole. They hedge even the smallest request heavily ("If it wouldn't be too much trouble..."). Their body language is like that of a cocker spaniel puppy—wide-eyed, smiling, and affectionate. They use "I/you" words a lot and are vocally expressive. A typical Placating utterance is "Sure, SURE, whatever YOU'D like is perfectly FINE with ME!"

Computing

People in the Computer mode use generalizations and abstractions rather than personal references ("Generally, what's done is..." or "The bottom line here is..."). They try to relay emotionless, neutral messages ("The fact of the matter is..." rather than "I feel..."). They use minimal body language: they're poker-faced, have a flat tone of voice, and gesture very little. A typical Computer utterance is: "Let's not react emotionally. Let's understand the basic principles and establish precise standard operating procedures here."

Distracting

People in a Distractor mode don't want to face the disagreement directly, so they skip from one approach to another ("This makes sense… On the other hand… Oh, who knows?") They may joke about the conflict or talk at length about minor, tangential issues—apparently forgetting the major issue that's still unresolved. Often they seem disorganized, even panicked, as if they don't know how they want to proceed. Sometimes they cycle between several of the other modes, at first Blaming, then Placating, then Computing. A typical Distracting utterance might be: "I can't believe you did this! But I'm sure you had a good reason. Oh, Lord, what'll we do now? Let's figure this out. I'll never forget the time this happened at my other firm…"

Leveling

Leveling is telling the truth about what you perceive, think, or feel to the best extent possible. It calls for facing a situation as directly and as personally as you can. The Leveler breaks through facades to get at what's really happening and why. Leveling may involve revealing the hidden agenda ("What I really think about this issue…" or "To be very frank, it seems to me…"). Leveler utterances vary a great deal. In fact, Leveling is characterized best by the *absence* of the other modes—there's no faultfinding, fault-avoiding, or evasion of the feelings or real issues involved.

Exercise 9:
Communication Modes

When you talk with the person who exhibits the difficult behavior you identified in Exercise 3, which of these five communication modes does that person use most often?

_____

_____

_____

_____

_____

_____

_____

Which do you use?

_____

_____

_____

_____

_____

_____

_____

RESPONSE STRATEGIES

In *Success With the Gentle Art of Verbal Self-Defense,*
Suzette Haden Elgin suggests several strategies that can be
useful for responding to difficult people who frequently use
one of the communication modes just described. Among her
suggestions:

- Decide whether you want to encourage or discourage
  the other person's mode of responding. Choose *your*
  response mode accordingly.

- Be general and abstract rather than personal if you're not
  sure how to respond.

- Implement the mode you feel is most appropriate.

Each of these responses is discussed in detail in the following
paragraphs.

Like Begets Like

The first strategy is based on the principle that *anything you
feed will grow.* Communication is a feedback loop. In other
words, like begets like. If you respond in the same mode as
the difficult person or *match* the other person's approach,
here's what will happen:

- Blaming someone who is blaming you will create a
  confrontation.

- Placating someone who is placating you creates a wishy-
  washy "After you," "No, after you" two-step and results
  in an undignified delay.

- Computing with someone who is computing also creates
  a two-step, except the delay appears far more dignified
  and significant.

- Distracting when someone else also is distracting builds avoidance on top of avoidance, creating a growing sense of panic.

- Leveling with someone who is leveling with you— sending the simple truth both ways—generally leads to greater mutual understanding, compromise, and new ideas for solving the problem.

So, your first decision is whether the mode the difficult person is using is something you want to encourage. If it is, match that mode. Otherwise, choose another mode for responding.

When in Doubt, Be a Computer

When you don't know which mode to choose, maintain the Computer mode until you have enough information to make a reasoned choice.

Why?

Many times people are triggered into their habitual mode because they feel extreme stress. They are upset and not consciously aware of what they are doing. As a reflex, they automatically start blaming, placating, distracting, or disclosing. And they'll do this consistently when they feel scared.

What do they fear?

- When people feel helpless or powerless, they snap into the Blamer mode to regain their loss of control.

- When people fear others will be angry and reject them, they snap into the Placater mode to regain their approval.

- When people feel alarmed by the intensity of their own or others' emotions, they snap into the Computer mode in an attempt to bury those emotions.

- When people have no idea how they feel about a situation, they snap into the Distractor mode to avoid taking a stand of any kind.

- When people cannot tolerate the vagueness or phoniness of a situation, they snap into the Leveling mode to bring real feelings and issues out in the open.

You should maintain the Computer mode just long enough to gather your thoughts and assess the situation. Shifting temporarily into that mode allows you to avoid impulsively making an inappropriate move. It provides a momentary respite while you consciously decide on your preferred mode.

Implement Your Preferred Mode

When you sense which mode is most appropriate for the situation at hand, you can strategically choose and implement it. How do you decide which mode is best?

First, you need to know, as certainly as you can, the mode of the other person. If, for example, someone says, "I'll go along with whatever you suggest," you should take a moment to assess whether the person is in a Placater or a Leveler mode.

If in a Placater mode, the person is temporarily trying to regain your good graces—not genuinely empty of opinions and ready to go along with what you propose. Once the person no longer fears upsetting you, he or she is likely to voice a preference, be annoyed with the decision you made, and subtly sabotage it.

If in a Leveler mode, however, the person's willingness to support your proposal is genuine and you can advocate and implement your idea.

How can you tell which mode you're facing? Elgin suggests this: "Watch for mismatch. The clash between the words and the body language of the speaker, as well as the way the intonation differs from normal stress patterns, will always give you the necessary clues."

When most people speak, they deliver up to 90 percent of their emotional information through nonverbal cues. And the most revealing aspect of nonverbal communication is the voice: its quality, tone, and intonation.

You may not realize it, but every day you make decisions and interpret messages based on the nonverbal clues that other people send. These nonverbal clues can also help you determine the communication mode a person is using. Let's examine again the example of differentiating Leveling from Placating messages. Test your ability to make this distinction in the following way: Imagine you're going out for the evening with someone whose tastes in entertainment differ dramatically from yours (he loves horror films, you prefer comedies; she likes steak, you're a vegetarian). Next, imagine you want this person's approval very much, and you fear the evening will be ruined unless you go along with what he or she wants. Down deep you resent this selfishness, but for the time being you're willing to indulge it in order to make the evening work. From this Placater frame of mind, say aloud, "I'll go along with whatever you suggest."

Next, imagine it's another occasion—you're about to go out with a friend (also with dissimilar tastes) who will be entering the hospital the next day for a life-threatening operation. You genuinely want this evening to be delightful for your partner and you want to indulge his or her every whim. From this Leveling frame of mind, say again, "I'll go along with whatever you suggest."

Can you hear the difference in your tone of voice? Did you notice any differences in your posture, facial expression, or gestures? You probably had little difficulty detecting the difference between the modes you used in those two identical utterances. (You might ask a friend to read the preceding section and repeat the exercise, not telling you which mode he or she is using first. You'll probably have little difficulty detecting the actual mode.)

Once you know the other person's mode, you can choose your own. Remember the basic principle that anything you feed will grow. So, if you want:

- A *delay,* use the Computer or Distractor mode.

- *To make the decision yourself,* first use the Placater mode to trigger a Placater response in the other person, and then decide.

- *The other person to decide,* just level and say so.

- *The conversation to be honest,* shift to the Leveling mode yourself.

Knowing about and recognizing communication modes is very helpful when you deal with difficult people. Many systems exist for categorizing individuals into one type of "character" or another. (See the first chapter of this book for a discussion of the system Robert Bramson describes in *Coping With Difficult People.*) But you as well as others are likely to shift from one communication mode to another depending on the demands of your situation. Managing difficult communication modes is preferable to labeling yourself or another person permanently as a particular type of character. Consider communication modes as different dance steps you can shift into when the music changes. Don't assume that you or anyone else dances to the same tune all the time.

Encouraging Desirable Behavior

There are two ways to manage difficult people. One is to decrease their difficult behavior. The other is to increase the behavior we approve of. We do the former more often: we notice and criticize shortcomings. We "catch" others doing something wrong. Too often, unfortunately, we take for granted and overlook all there is to appreciate and encourage.

I AM IN TOTAL CONTROL! DO EXACTLY AS I SAY AND NO ONE WILL GET HURT!

TRACKING POSITIVES

People respond better to praise than to criticism. They are willing to work harder for someone who recognizes and appreciates what they do well than for someone who picks at whatever they do.

But you may think: "People won't change or improve unless their shortcomings are pointed out. Praise only entrenches the status quo."

Not necessarily. One international pharmaceutical company, for example, uses a program called "Tracking Positives" to train its salespeople. Here's how it works.

The instructor explains the selling skills the company wants its salespeople to use. The trainees work in pairs to practice selling the company's products to each other. Observers look for "positives"—desirable behaviors.

Following each practice round, the observers track the positives of each salesperson, pointing out all the behaviors they believe will make that salesperson successful. No one mentions any negative or undesirable behaviors.

During each round, trainees have opportunities to practice selling and to track the positives of other trainees. Between rounds, the positives from the preceding rounds are reviewed, and trainees are encouraged to maintain them. An additional skill to practice is also identified.

The participants feel appreciated and encouraged. Their self-confidence increases, and they enjoy learning. They learn from observing others' good points. And they avoid the embarrassment and inhibition that critical feedback usually causes. The instructors insist on tracking only positives because they consider it an efficient way to teach.

But you don't have to be teaching in order to track positives. If you tell other people what pleases you about their behavior, they will enjoy their work more, enjoy being around you, and feel more motivated to do things for you. Simply put, try to catch people doing something right.

Think of someone you consider "difficult." In Exercise 10, list three very specific things that person did in the last week that you *liked*. Some examples might be:

- "Told me honestly what he thought"
- "Apologized when he made a mistake"
- "Left me alone to do the job my own way"

Exercise 10:
Tracking Positives

Here are three *desirable* behaviors that a person I consider difficult has performed in the last week:

1. _____

_____

_____

_____

_____

_____

2. _____

_____

_____

_____

_____

_____

3. _____

_____

_____

_____

_____

_____

CONVEYING PRAISE MESSAGES

Next, let's examine the ways you can convey that a desirable behavior pleases you. In *Winning Ways to Succeed With People,* Helen Hall Clinard identifies the following nonverbal communication, words, and actions that people use to express appreciation:

Nonverbal Communication	Words	Actions
Smiling	Saying "thank you"	Giving a gift
Nodding	Telling someone else about it	Buying a drink
Waving	Requesting that it be done again	Presenting an award
Giving a thumbs up	Saying "good," "bravo," "terrific"	Inviting the person to lunch
Clasping and raising hands	Praising the person	Increasing responsibilities
Shaking hands	Giving a message of appreciation	Designating a new job title
Giving a pat on the back		Behaving similarly

These methods of expressing appreciation aren't applicable in all situations. They are merely alternatives for letting someone know that you are aware of a particular behavior and like it.

Now, look back at the list of three "positives" you identified in Exercise 10. Did you let that person know you noticed and liked each one?

If not, look again at Clinard's list. Which of the ways listed could you have used? Which will you use the next time that person does something positive?

Granted, giving praise isn't always easy or even desirable, especially to someone who usually is difficult. Praise sometimes is perceived as insincere, patronizing, false, manipulative, "a way of buttering someone up," breeding complacency, or raising false expectations. No wonder people underuse praise!

But if used properly, praise can be effective. What makes the difference between praise that works and praise that backfires?

- *Sincerity.* You must genuinely believe that what you are praising is a "positive." Avoid phony praise!

- *Specificity.* Your praise must be concrete, not vague. "I found your report easy to follow" is much more specific than "Good job on the report." Specific messages are helpful and believable.

- *Disclosure vs. Evaluation.* Praise that describes your personal experience is better than praise that evaluates the other person. (Compare again the two praise messages in the last paragraph.) If you're not an expert on the kind of behavior you're praising, your evaluation may be inaccurate or unappreciated.

Effective praising, therefore, clearly states:

- The specific behavior you like.

- How this behavior is helpful.

- How you feel as a result of this help.

Imagine that you are an employee who stayed late one night to help your boss meet an important deadline.

What's the specific behavior? Staying after hours on Tuesday night to help complete a project.

How was this behavior helpful? The boss was able to meet the deadline.

How does the boss feel? Relieved and grateful.

Imagine that you received this message of praise from your boss:

> "I really appreciate your staying late to help me Tuesday night. I was very relieved to get the project done properly and sent off on time. I couldn't have done either without you."

Would you:

- Know the specific behavior your boss appreciates?

- Know how the behavior was useful to her?

- Know how she felt about it?

- Believe the sincerity of the message?

- Feel more positive about yourself?

- Feel more positive about her?

- Feel motivated to continue or repeat the behavior?

If your answer was "yes" to most or all of these questions, you can see the importance of each element.

Exercise 11:

Messages of Praise

Take a minute now to write out an equivalent message of praise relating to any one of the three "positives" you identified for your "difficult" person in Exercise 10.

_____

_____

_____

_____

_____

_____

_____

_____

_____

_____

_____

_____

_____

_____

_____

_____

MAKE IT A HABIT

You may think that following the "formula" proposed here is out of place and awkward in interpersonal relationships. You may value spontaneity and sincerity in your communication with people and fear that following this formula would interfere more than help.

Of course, artificiality can kill communication as easily as a vague, judgmental message. But keep in mind that spontaneity is dependent on habits. We spontaneously do things that are motivated by feelings and flow from habit.

Habits are based on practice. Habitually doing what doesn't work just gets you deeper into hot water. The period of initial awkwardness you will experience until you've consciously used a new behavior frequently enough to make it a habit is a worthwhile investment of your energy.

Actually, tracking positives with messages of appreciation is a relatively easy and risk-free way to deal with difficult people. Although some people may at first view your positive messages with skepticism, they will soon learn to value your appreciation if you are sincere, and you will gradually develop a more satisfactory and productive relationship.

THE CONDITIONAL
APPRECIATION MESSAGE

Say your difficult person really isn't "out to get you." In fact, the person wants to please you, but he or she isn't doing a good job of it right now.

You might have to wait a long time for the desired behavior to occur (perhaps by accident) before you can affirm it. However, by varying the standard appreciation message slightly, you can encourage the behavior you want *before* it occurs. Simply describe the specific behavior you *would* like, how it *would* help you, and how you *would* feel about it. Here are some examples:

> *"Jack, I'd appreciate a week's notice before the next report is needed. That allows me to gather accurate and up-to-date information without feeling rushed. Doing it that way would be much more pleasant for me and provide better results."*

> *"Fay, I'd appreciate your putting these files in alphabetical order for me so I can access them more easily."*

> *"Jean, would you come in a half hour early tomorrow morning so we can set up the room and go over the agenda for the directors' meeting? I would feel more comfortable about the meeting if those things are taken care of ahead of time. That way, we will be free to greet everyone as they arrive."*

These *conditional appreciation messages* contain the same three elements as appreciation messages, but they are based on the *condition* that a desired behavior will occur rather than on one that has already occurred. These conditional messages are recommended when the "difficult" person wants to do what pleases you but does not know what that is.

Exercise 12:
Conditional Appreciation Messages

Select one of the difficult behaviors you listed in Exercise 2. Using the guidelines for conditional appreciation messages, write a message asking the person to behave in the way you prefer.

_____

_____

_____

_____

_____

_____

_____

_____

_____

_____

_____

_____

_____

_____

_____

_____

_____

Summing
It Up

To summarize, "difficult people" often turn out not to be so difficult after all *if* you:

- Make an effort to change their behavior.

- Maintain a good working relationship.

- Examine your own contribution to the difficult behavior pattern.

- Are flexible in your communication modes.

- Encourage desirable behaviors.

When you deal with a difficult person, remember this comment from a novel by Russian author Maxim Gorky:

> "Everybody, my friend, everybody lives for something better to come. That's why we want to be considerate of every man. Who knows what's in him, why he was born, and what he can do!"

Bibliography

Alberti, Robert E., and Michael L. Emmons. *Stand Up, Speak Out, Talk Back!* New York: Pocket Books, 1975.

Alberti, Robert E., and Michael L. Emmons. *Your Perfect Right.* San Luis Abispo, CA: Impact Publishers, 1990.

Bach, George R., and Ronald M. Deutsch. *Stop! You're Driving Me Crazy.* New York: Berkley Books, 1979.

Berry, Carmen R. *When Helping You Is Hurting Me.* New York: Harper Collins, 1988.

Blanchard, Kenneth, and Spencer Johnson. *The One Minute Manager.* New York: Berkley Books, 1982.

Bolton, Robert. *People Skills: How to Assert Yourself, Listen to Others, and Resolve Conflicts.* New York: Simon and Schuster, 1979.

Bowen, Donald. "Self-Annihilating Games in Interpersonal Relations," *Journal of Teaching Behavior* 10(3): 31-44.

Bramson, Robert M. *Coping With Difficult People.* New York: Ballantine Books, 1981.

Carnegie, Dale. *How to Win Friends and Influence People.* New York: Pocket Books, 1964.

Carter, Jay. *Nasty People: How to Stop Being Hurt by Them Without Becoming One of Them.* Chicago: Contemporary Books, 1979.

Clinard, Helen Hall. *Winning Ways to Succeed With People.* Houston: Gulf Publishing, 1985.

Elgin, Suzette Haden. *Success With the Gentle Art of Verbal Self-Defense.* Englewood Cliffs, NJ: Prentice Hall, 1989.

Fisher, Roger, and Scott Brown. *Getting Together: Building a Relationship That Gets to Yes.* Boston: Houghton-Mifflin, 1988.

Hauck, Paul A. *How to Stand Up for Yourself.* Philadelphia: Westminster Press, 1979.

Hochheiser, Robert M. *How to Work for a Jerk.* New York: Vintage Books, 1987.

Kaplan, R.E., W.H. Drath, and J.R. Kofomides. *High Hurdles: The Challenge of Executive Self-Development,* Tech. Rep. No. 25. Greensboro, SC: Center for Creative Leadership, 1985.

McGinnis, Alan Loy. *Bringing out the Best in People.* Minneapolis: Augsburg Publishing, 1989.

Miller, George A. "Giving Away Psychology in the 80's," *Psychology Today* (January 1980): 38.

Monroe, Craig, Mark Borzoi, and Vincent DiSalvo. "Conflict Behaviors of Difficult Subordinates," *The Southern Communication Journal* 54 (April 1989): 311-329.

Satir, Virginia. *The New Peoplemaking.* Mountain View, CA: Science and Behavior Books, 1988.

Terkel, Studs. *Working: People Talk About What They Do All Day and How They Feel About What They Do.* New York: Pantheon, 1974.

Select from these SkillPath Books for Your Professional and Personal Growth

Title	Item Number

Handbooks

A Winning Attitude:	12-0009
How to Develop Your Most Important Asset!	
Breaking The Ice	12-0012
How To Improve Your On-The-Spot Communication Skills	
Dynamic Delegation!	12-0010
A Manager's Guide For Active Empowerment	
Every Woman's Guide to Career Success	12-0003
Hiring and Firing:	12-0008
What Every Manager Needs to Know	
How to Deal With Difficult People	12-0004
Meetings That Work	12-0006
Networking:	12-0011
How to Creatively Tap Your People Resources	
Power Write!	12-0002
A Practical Guide to Words That Work	
Taking Charge:	12-0005
A Personal Guide to Managing Projects and Priorities	
The Supervisor's Guide	12-0001
The Everyday Guide to Coordinating People and Tasks	

Self-Study Sourcebooks

Total Quality Customer Service	13-0004
How To Make It Your Way of Life	
Productivity Power:	13-0002
250 Great Ideas for Being More Productive	
Risk-Taking:	13-0003
50 Ways To Turn Risks Into Rewards	
Write It Right!	13-0001
A Guide for Clear and Correct Writing	

To order any of these resources, or to request a complete SkillPath BookStore catalog, call toll-free **1-800-873-7545** or **1-913-677-3200**.